Holy, Holey, Wholly?

a journey of
faith and
perspective

Holy, Holey, Wholly?

a journey of
faith and
perspective

Julie
Barricklow

Published by BookLocker.com, Inc., Bradenton, Florida.

Cover Design: Julie Barricklow/Scot McKim
Cover Photo: Julie Barricklow
ISBN 978-0-692-25070-9

Library of Congress Control Number: 2014913522

Printed on acid-free paper.

Booklocker.com, Inc.
2015

First Edition

To family and friends who walked with me on this journey, especially Jennifer, Raye, Bob, Scot, Trish, and the NCF family.
Thank you for traveling with me.

To you, Papa, for always being there, even when I look away.
May Your Glory be seen in these pages.

Contents

Look at the cover. Where do you see yourself in this image? Are you the stone, chiseled, set, guiding/containing the stream? The water, falling, hitting the hard surface, merging with other drops to drift on? Or maybe you are the question mark, undefined, hazy, hovering over the water, not quite sure where you fit in the picture.

In my journey with God over the past few years, I've seen myself through all these perspectives and continue to challenge myself, to change, to see from new angles. I enjoy discovering Him in the details around me. From an afternoon walk in a garden to an evening campfire, I'm constantly surprised at where and how He chooses to meet me.

Some questions I pose here encourage you to explore, question, even discount these viewpoints. May they open to you new perspectives on who God is, His purpose, and how we were created to bring Him glory.

Julie Barricklow

Dove Flight

A dove was protecting, comforting, sitting with one of its young who had flown from the nest. The young dove's world had changed drastically in a fledgling flight. New perspective, scary prospects. But its parent was by its side, encouraging it, keeping it warm, sharing company.

You, oh Lord, are like that dove. Your wings are ever covering me, encouraging me. I have been reborn with Your dove sight and Your wings. You have given me the ability to fly, and I am trying out these new wings. I have landed in a scary place, but You are still around, watching, encouraging me to fly. *"Try, try, try,"* you keep telling me, *"Don't give up."*

You tell me when to hide, when to blend in, but also when to strive to fly, to change my perspective, my view of the world. This is Your plan all along, to have me soar to new heights, to new places. You call to me, *"Don't be afraid, my daughter. I have you. I will not let you fall. Just like the fledgling, you must learn to fly. You have to try those wings. I am."*

Change

A new year begins, so I come to You, asking what Your will is for me. In order to change, I must move. Treading water is wearing me out. I need to either climb onto the bank or strike out for the distant shore.

You have equipped me to take the journey, so why do I hesitate? You have never let me down before. Am I willing to go the distance? Am I willing to get uncomfortable, and if so, how much? My will continually shoves itself to the foreground, trying to remain the focus.

Whatever I choose, You will equip me to perform to the best You have given me. Papa, help me be bold in my movement, that it may be one with Your desire and will for me. Take these hands and show me their purpose. Take my mind and show me the ideas that You have.

Creativity all around me, I need only to look up and be graced by Your sky. Seeing the glorious sunsets, pink feather clouds, and the ice rainbows are amazing! What an abundance You show me! May Your blessing flow off me onto others. Drench them in the deluge that is Your extravagant love!

Streams

Have you ever felt God's presence around you? I'm not talking about the theological "God is all around us" explanation. I'm talking about His quiet presence, that déjà vu moment around others.

This past summer, I experienced such a contemplative moment. I imagined Him walking among the group I was with, connecting us through multiple experiences, challenging us in simple conversation, opening up doors of thought and life choices we'd never been aware of, bridging the chasms of fear and insecurity that we were standing on the brink of. It was peacefully amazing.

Through an engaging discussion with a dynamic young man, I had the strong impression that Jesus was talking with me. I delighted in his quiet conversation and was amazed how loud he was at certain points without even raising his tone. I realized during this talk that I needed to take a chance, that God would meet me, hold me, keep me from going under.

I should not forget what I have experienced so far, but I do need to move on, using the past as a reference to some degree. If I try to duplicate what I've been through, even if it was good, I deny myself the opportunity of something new, something possibly better.

Think for a moment of a woodland stream. As it flows past a rock, it doesn't say, "I don't want to go this way anymore. I'm going to flow past the tree instead." Streams don't decide to change on their own. They are shaped by outside influences — a flood, a fallen tree, human impact.

Change happens in all aspects of life. How I respond to it is up to me. Will I allow this event to stop my forward motion, or do I jump in wearing my Jesus PFD (personal flotation device) and exclaim, "Wonder what's coming next?"

Frozen

I am a mess. I feel so fragile. My feelings are all over the place. I've kept my heart frozen in protection from hurt, woe, and pain. In my struggle, I cry out to You, Papa! Pour Your flames of love down on this icy heart! Only by melting it down, liquefying it, evaporating it, can my transformation occur.

I can't change these boundaries I've placed around my heart, but You can. Only through Your searingly hot outpouring, cleansing me, purifying me, can I know the change is taking place. It's hard to let go of the so-called control I have on my heart. Continue until only Your flames are left and I am naught. Through this process I am released!

A Walk with My Beloved

I took a walk today with my Beloved. He led me through a beautiful, crisp fall afternoon at a nature preserve. The trails, covered with fallen leaves, crunched underfoot. The cool breeze and the scents of the woods brought back childhood memories of playing in leaf-pile nests.

I enjoy fall the most and my Beloved knows that. Surrounded by the dying of living things, there is such incredible beauty. Such life to be found in the decay of the leaves! I've recently had to allow some feelings toward others to die. I keep reaching out to those feelings, those connections, wondering if there is any hope of reviving those areas of my life again. Just as I ask the question, God shows me a new perspective on those emotions. New life is present through the death of those feelings, a new beauty unseen before.

Change is inevitable. I know God, my Beloved, my true Love, has better things in store for me. Flooding my senses with smells and sights of happy times, He reminds me of what was in my life. His gentle invitation to go on a walk with Him is a simple request, enabling Him to show me what He is doing in it presently. How can I resist an offer like that?

Baggage

Do not take along any gold or silver or copper in your belts; take no bag for the journey, or extra tunic, or sandals or a staff; for the worker is worth his keep.

Matthew 10:9, 10

Baggage. Oh how we travel! Day trips, week-long vacations. All have one thing in common. Baggage. We always have something to take with us, hence baggage. Whether a small backpack or a 3-piece luggage set, we fill them with items we know we need. Or, in my case, things I might use.

As a Girl Scout, being prepared is a part of my process to journey. I pack things that most others wouldn't consider. Band-aids, duct tape, a mini flashlight, cough drops, a lighter, and playing cards are stock items I keep in the backpack I take on trips. You just never know when you might need something odd.

This causes me to pause and think about the preparations I make for the trips I take inside myself. The journeys of the heart, mind, spirit. It's harder to anticipate these destinations than an external trip, so I gather up feelings, experiences, and hurts and pack them into my mind. I bring more than I need, because I never know what crisis might arise where I would need to drag out some offense or feeling from the past. Does this sound familiar? I wish I could say I don't do this very often, but that would be far from the truth.

Why do I carry this burdensome, awkward, and sometimes painful junk around? Why am I more comfortable with these loads instead of their absences? Like the weighty backpack, it seems easier to just haul the emotional stuff around instead of dumping it and continuing without it. Give up my baggage? Do I look like I'm having trouble wading through this swamp with this large Samsonite on my shoulders? What, there's an alligator coming my way? Wouldn't it be easier (and better for my life) if I just dropped the whole mess and high-tailed it out of there? Yes!!!

Jesus sent out the disciples, instructing them not to take anything with them. He told them they didn't need baggage. Whatever was needed for their journey would be provided on their way. I believe this refers not only to physical but mental baggage also. The use of baggage is a choice. I can choose to take it or leave it. After being bowed over from carrying weighty items, it's hard to stand up straight after they are gone, but it is possible with help from God. I'm choosing to leave 'em and make for higher ground!

Choices

My thoughts were of you, my friend, yesterday as I traveled. I care for you deeply, but do I show God's love to you? I enjoy being with you because you challenge me in so many ways. You have exposed me to more of the world, and because of that, I have another way of looking at things around me. Because of you, I've become more involved in the community around me and helping others who can use my skills.

You might think this newfound involvement would cause me to wander away from my faith, weakening my resolve in the relationship I have with Jesus. NO! It has brought me closer, deepened my commitment, expanded my love for my Savior by loving on those around me!

I wish you could share in this love I have for Him. It saddens me to see you reach out and work so hard for something you believe in, only to have it fizzle and fade before your eyes. I hear in our discussions that your expectations for situations are great, but reality doesn't meet your hopes.

How frustrated do you have to become before you change your behavior, your choices? You keep doing the same things and getting the same results. Do you want to change? Are you tired of living the same old life, day-in and day-out?

When are you going to let God give you a new heart? When He does, He <u>will</u> fill it to overflowing. Do you really want to settle for less than the best He has for you?

Are you truly satisfied with where you are? What I hear from you doesn't sound like it. What are you willing to do about it? Will you switch focus, tactics, choices, and <u>risk</u> what might be your breakthrough? What will be your choice?

Risk

With a sharp intake of breath, I timidly place my feet in the cold water: cool, refreshing, jarring. After the initial shock, the mountain-fed stream takes away my other thoughts, leaving only the focus of immediate discomfort. The subtle bite of cold starts at the toes. How much more can I take? Sometimes I can go until there is nothing but numbness.

Right now, though, the pain is becoming too much. I remove my feet from the water, allowing the discomfort to eke away. When feeling has once again returned, I stick them back into the bracing flow. The movement, the coolness is too appealing to resist.

I have to risk the pain for the feeling of relief. But push it too far, and I dare going numb. The anticipation is gone, I cannot feel the flowing water. How often do I immerse myself in the cold stream of life? After the initial shock, I tolerate the icy bitterness. But then the pain of cold moves in, chilling, stabbing, forcing my next move.

Do I stay in and slowly, excruciatingly succumb to the numbness, or do I step back out onto the sandbar to regain the precious feeling of life flowing through me?

Some are resigned to give up, to put the shoes and socks back on and walk away. Some stay, frozen in time, numbed beyond movement and the return of life-giving blood. Then there's the group that, after a brief respite, slowly re-enters the stream once again to discover a new place to stand, maybe wander upstream, listening, while waiting for the cold to come.

The voice of God can be heard in the flow, the jumble of gurgles and burbles. Multiple octaves speak at once, yet none overpower. A harmonious cacophony of nature speaks to my soul, my spirit, as I re-enter the water. God washes over me, asks me to venture out further, to step into the wonder of Him. Rest, refresh, and risk at the same time.

Words

God, I love you. I love you. Jesus, I love you. Spirit, I love you. I can't say it enough, I Love You!

Words. Where do they take me? Down what roads do they steer me? How quickly I travel when hearing certain words, tones, phrases. I'm carried, swept away, run over with them. Talk about efficient vehicles! They come in all shapes and sizes. Some are racy, flashy, colorful and send me spinning, dizzy, light-headed. Others are plain, non-descript, middle of the road. Oh, how we trust these modes of transportation!

I often walk alone with my words, moving to my own tempo, to get to a destination of thought. Every now and again, a bus pulls up beside me. It seems like a convenient way to travel. Fellow travelers heading in the same direction with someone else in charge, driving the bus. Do I choose to get on? It depends on who's driving. (And don't we all drive buses sometimes in our lives?)

A friend opened up my eyes to these choices. If negative words are being thrown around, and edification and positive thoughts are tossed out the window, what am I going to do? In her words, "I'm not getting on <u>that</u> bus!"

How often am I exposed to words, thoughts, feelings of others? Every day! And where do they take me? Where do I end up? Am I downfallen, trodden upon? How about angry, vicious, vengeful? Or maybe, just possibly, I see a ray of hope, a drop of sunshine, a pearl of promise.

Not all buses that present themselves are disheartening. Words of encouragement, of love, of belief can carry me further, faster, to my destination of thought. They can take me to a place that is enjoyable to be in, a secure location.

The next time I travel down a conversation, turn a corner, and find a bus, a carrier of words/feelings/thoughts, I'll stop and reflect. Where is it going? Am I going to enjoy where I end up? And more importantly, who's driving? It might be you.

Dancing

May I have this dance?

    I don't know how to dance.

That is not what I asked. May I have this dance?

    But I don't know how.

Do you trust me?

    Yes.

Then, may I have this dance?

    I want to, but I'm afraid of making a fool of myself.

You won't be a fool. We will take one step at a time. No more, no less. Do you still trust me?

    Yes.

Come then and dance with me. I will be gentle and patient as you learn. All you have to do is take my hand. Will you come and dance with me? I promise not to let go of your hands, just follow my lead. Just listen to the music. Is it not wonderful? Have you heard anything like it before? It's full of life, and speaks of love, and offers the promises of forever. I will be by you and will catch you if you stumble. It's okay to stumble. That's how you learn. So . . . take a deep breath.

(deep breath)
May I have this dance?
Yes, you may.

Roller Coaster

I'm a classic roller coaster fan. What I mean by classic is your sit-down, thrills-and-spills, wooden roller coaster. As a child, I remember visits to my grandparents in southern Indiana. Dad would drive the "back way" to treat us to the dips and turns of the country roads. How I loved flying over those hills just to feel my stomach drop! Dad knew the best places (for maximum effect) since he grew up there. Of course, this was all before seatbelts were required. Part of the thrill was flying up in the air, defying gravity for a split second.

I feel my life has been spent on various roller coasters. Lots of ups and downs, twists and turns, and the occasional upside-down loop-the-loop. I look at a situation and think about the ride that I'm on. Every day I'm faced with new challenges, old arguments, persistent questions of where I am or where I'm going.

Some of these experiences leave me up in the air, and some twist me around so tight I can't seem to gain my balance. Some days I wish I hadn't gotten on this particular ride. It's rough; it throws me around, beats me up, shakes me 'til my teeth rattle. (Ever been on one of those rides before?) But then I come up and over the last small hill and coast into the station. Ahhh, a break at last! The safety bar lifts and I can climb out of the car. But now I'm faced with a dilemma. Do I go back through the line and get on again, or do I choose to not ride for a while? (Was it really worth it?)

My choice hinges on who is in charge of this particular ride. When I look up into the control station, who do I see there? Is it me or is it God, my forever Papa? When He is running the ride, I know I'll be okay. He'll make sure my safety bar is always down, locked in place. I know there will be twists and turns, but He monitors the speed and doesn't allow the car to go any faster than I can handle.

These factors alone make the ride worthwhile. If I trust Him completely with my life, I'm promised a ride that is thrilling, stomach-dropping, reminiscent of the childhood rides with my earthly father. I'm given the freedom to hang onto the bar and grin, or throw my arms up and yell with delight.

How gratifying it is to see His shining face, grinning joyfully from ear to ear, as I coast back into the station. Glancing at the seat next to me, I see Jesus sitting there, looking just as pumped as I am! WOW!!! I've **GOT** to keep remembering God won't send me on a ride by myself. I always have someone to grip hands with, hang onto, join in my screams of glee. Our Papa rejoices when He sees us together. This is what He planned.

As the master coaster designer, He knows what will happen at every curve. After I pass a section, He alters, tweaks, changes the tracks so the next go round will present itself anew. Who wants to ride the same ride over and over and over again?

As I start to get bored, anticipating the hills and curves previously enjoyed, I REALLY get tired of the areas I don't like! Nope, sign me up for the ever-changing coaster. My God, who is constant, true, never changing, is a God of new things, of hope, a firm expectation of change. Right now, I need some change in my life.

Sojourning

Contentment is not freedom from desire, but freedom of desire. Being content is not pretending that everything is the way you wish it to be; it is not acting as though you have no wishes. Rather, it is no longer being ruled by your desires.

At this point in our journey, we have only three options: (1) to be alive and thirsty, (2) to be dead, or (3) to be addicted. Most of the world lives in addiction; most of the church has chosen deadness.

John Eldridge
Desire

Where am I? Am I a pilgrim? Am I sojourning? The word 'pilgrim' can be defined as a religious devotee who journeys to a shrine or sacred place, or one who embarks on a quest for something conceived of as sacred. Huh. Here I thought it was one of those people who wore black and white and funny hats and landed at Plymouth Rock (loose

27

interpretation of Webster's final definition). But the word itself derives from the alteration of the Latin *pereginus*, meaning 'foreigner.'

Now the word 'sojourn' means to reside temporarily, a brief period of residence. Interesting. When I think about where I am, I truly am a pilgrim (a foreigner), sojourning (temporarily residing) in this world, on a quest, a journey to a sacred place, the place of my desire. I must stay alive, thirst for more, to continue the journey. How eager I become when I know the place I long to be is around the corner, over the hill, in the next room. I must remind myself I'm only here for a short time. Even as these words fall on the page, I can see a glimpse of what is to come.

Come, fellow sojourner, continue to walk. For as pilgrims, we need remember that the lands where we reside must be left behind to continue the journey. Be not afraid, for we travel together. And as such partners do, we encourage each other when we falter. So, up, up, take another step! Here, take another sip until we arrive at our final destination, our desire!

Awake or Asleep?

Many days, I go through my usual routine without pause. I just coast through, not concerned or aware of what is happening. Then I hit a speed bump, a snag in my schedule, an unexpected glitch. Oh, the frustration! I grumble and gnash my teeth. (Ever wonder what that sounds like? I believe it's the noise of teeth grinding together while grumbling.)

In some cases, there are things I could have done differently to improve the outcome. In others, situations were beyond my grasp. It would be so easy to lay the blame in God's lap, to ask Him where He was during these times, to ask if He was asleep during these occurrences.

I recall the story of Jesus asleep in a boat during a storm. The disciples, terrified, woke Him. He then calmed the storm, as if this happened regularly. I think about His stillness, His ability to rest in the midst of that storm. When I'm hit by the storms in my life, rest is at the bottom of my priorities.

I wonder what would happen if I did rest during these times? Gnashing doesn't seem to solve my problems: it only causes my jaw to hurt.

I believe it's time for me to change my course of action and take a break. When the next storm blows in, I'll grab my pillow and a warm blanket and settle in for a good nap. God will take care of the storm. If He needs me, He knows where to find me.

Walking in the Dark

I enjoy walking in the dark, inside my house or out in the neighborhood. In my home, I can navigate pretty well without a light. Up fourteen steps, turn left, six steps and I'm at my bedroom door. Four more steps to the bedpost, three to the left and voila! My pillow beckons me. It's simple to move about in familiar territory in the dark. I know where everything is, except for the occasional dog toy.

One weekend, I was housesitting for my sister. I was fairly acquainted with her layout, or so I thought. I was working at the computer, in the dark, and stood up to get something. As I turned, I divided the toes of one foot with a chair leg. Oh, the agony of the feet!

This experience isn't far from my walk with God. After enlightening encounters, I come down from the mountain and continue my journey. Slowly, the glow around me begins to fade, and soon I'm making my way through the dark. Sure, it's hard to see, but after a time my eyes adjust to the dimness and away I go. Then, WHAM! An object that I didn't perceive is in my path.

Stubbed toes for sure, but what's my next move? I can slow down and make my way around this obstacle, or I can reach into my pocket and pull out the flashlight God gave me. God's Word is that flashlight in the dark. It doesn't immediately illuminate everything around me, but it does light a clear path to get around what's in my way with enough peripheral light to continue on the journey. Open the Bible and see how God shines, how He illuminates the obstacles in the darkness. It's been there all along, so why not use it?

Friendship

Friendship is a shelter, a comfort in the wind and rain. It is love poured out for the sake of love. It does not demand in return. If it receives in return, it rejoices and pours even more out. It can be tossed about in the storms of time, beaten, bruised, pulled at.

But if the foundation is true, storms strengthen it, not weaken it. Love is woven through it as a delicate strand of precious gold. And as gold is treasured, so is this gift that is given freely.

Friendship doesn't demand to be bowed to. Instead, it bows, it submits. The gift is set at the feet of those who want it, to be picked up and to be opened.

Exploration

Have you ever known someone who made you look at yourself? Who asked questions that made you dig deep down inside for the answer because you want your response to matter not only to you, but also to your friend?

A friend of mine does this with me. Our conversations range all over the place. Now and then, my friend poses a question that causes me to pause and really think about what has been asked. Most times, I rebut with questions of my own to better define what was asked. Then I answer.

I used to dislike these kinds of questions. Now I enjoy the exploration. It's a healthy quest that allows me to plum my knowledge, or lack thereof. It also enables me to see what my convictions are, where my choices have led me, to compare what I say to what I do.

Sometimes I come away from these discussions wondering what exactly we were talking about. I ask myself if I made a difference in my friend's life in the answering. Only God knows.

Questions

Where am I going? What am I doing with my life? What am I doing to achieve more? Questions fill me, surround me, overwhelm me with the fluttering buzzes of whispers. I don't want to ask, but I won't get answers unless I do.

Why do I hesitate so much? I'm afraid of the "no," the "not this time" responses that could push me over the edge, possibly dashing me on the rocks below. But I have hope and it is found in you, Papa.

You answer even when I don't hear the response. You send word to my head, my heart, my innermost being, that in good time, Your time, the answers will come. Having that hope allows the dreams to live, to thrive — a confirmation of tomorrow.

Perspective

Thoughts tumble over one another, begging to be released from my lips. Why is that? Why do they fight to get out? Is there a chance—albeit a small one—that when they are released, are spoken, they may receive life, continue to grow, and live?

I wish I could breathe life into some thoughts, but that isn't my arena. You are the Breath of Life. Only You can bring to life the thoughts running through my head. Some of them You choose to speak into existence. Most of them You listen to and say, "These are not what I want for you."

A lot of my thoughts are for Your ears only. They build up inside me, and if I don't release them, I'm afraid they'll escape when they shouldn't. Speaking them out loud to You is a safety valve that helps me keep Your perspective. I hear what I'm actually saying and realize how it sounds.

This, in turn, gives me the opportunity to evaluate the particular thought, allowing me to expand upon it or quash it. I also can hear Your response more clearly. I understand the circumstances more distinctly than before.

You grant me the ability to see my life, my situations, through Your eyes, Your heart. Your perspective causes me to pause and evaluate what I need to change. I realize how I need to shift my mind-set back to Your will. In doing so, I'm relieved of the anxiety I feel, the helplessness that seems to creep into my thoughts. You are my hope and will be forever. I know that.

Design

*Do you not know that your body is a
temple of the Holy Spirit, who is in you,
whom you have received from God?*

1 Corinthians 6:19

Some days I look in the mirror and wonder, *When did this
wrinkle appear? Boy, I look tired. I wish I could change this
feature in some way.* Then I read this verse and my
perspective changes.

In the Old Testament, David gave Solomon the plans
for building the temple. These were given to him by the
Spirit of the Lord, divine inspiration. God planned out every
detail of His house. Every measurement, every
ornamentation, even the weight of the gold and silver to be
used. Nothing was overlooked.

So, in my infinite wisdom (ha!), why do I criticize my
design? I, as a creation of God, am no less divinely
designed. If my body is a temple for Him to rest in, why do

I chafe at the design? The worldview that surrounds me tells me I can do better. How's that working for me? It's not.

God designed me the way I am for a purpose. Slowly, He is revealing new rooms inside me that I never knew about. In His creation, it's not just the external me that matters, but the internal, too.

There are days He shows me the whimsy, the creative ornamentation He has woven into my being. I delight in these glimpses. They remind me that even though I live in this body, I'm not the owner of the home. God's complete design is perfect in His eyes. I may not agree on some days, but who am I to argue with the Master Creator?

God is the consummate renovator — re-purposing rooms, changing layouts, removing outdated materials. He changes the physical body with age, but it's the interior changes that are the most dramatic.

He specifies in minute detail the plans for my heart, my soul, my spirit. It is His Holy of Holies, the place where He resides, and He can make it look however He wants. I'm honored and humbled that He chooses to do this every day for me.

So now, when I look in the mirror, I don't see someone who is getting older. I see the Holy of Holies, the place where my God has chosen to live. Just like a priest of old who entered unprepared into this sacred space, I have been put to death for entering. But through His High Priest, Jesus Christ, I am brought back to life, sanctified, granted entrance into His presence.

DNA Transfusion

While walking one evening, I was struck by how much I need God in my life. How much I need the sacrificial gift of Jesus' life for me. The sin in my life is a viral infection. Left alone, unchecked, it spreads, attacking area after area.

It attacks me in various forms, this sneaky, sinister illness. No treatment will take it away, only a transfusion. A donation of blood so pure, it will re-write my DNA, erasing the old me. Only blood of divinity, of eternity, can heal the insidious nature I've had growing inside of me.

When I accept this lifeblood, transfusion gives way to transformation, rebuilding the weakened and failing parts. Tired but still moving, I slowly take steps to regain strength, all the while leaning on my donor, my Jesus.

Full recovery in this life isn't possible; I'll never walk without His help. I'm not meant to. In all reality, who wants to walk alone in this life? As long as I hold onto His arm, I have a companion to talk to, listen to, laugh with, cry on, love forever. And I, in return, receive love. A partner for life and eternity.

Wait

Tonight, I sit on the front porch, watching, waiting as a spring thunderstorm comes in. The lightning jags across the sky, lighting it up with shades of faint blues and pinks. I count until the thunder rolls in.

Each bolt brings the storm closer. Water fills and overflows the gutters, splattering the sidewalk. The wind picks up a little, casting mist across my face. Still, I sit and watch, waiting. For what? I don't have the faintest idea.

As I sit, my mind tumbles, rumbles, through my day's activities. It jumps to an idea I've been struggling with, then to my solution. Pray. Why hadn't I thought of that before? Why did I think I could resolve this tiny detail without God's help? Sure, I could continue down the path I've chosen and crawl to a solution, but why would I want to? He listens to what I feel are my major problems, struggles, issues, so why not now?

Deep in my heart, I trust Him with my innermost desires, failings, secrets. Isn't He the God of things both large and small? Yes! If I want to move more in Him and have His direction to guide me, I must ask, declare, voice my call for help, even with the small, insignificant, miniscule details that run rampant through my thought processes.

So I will continue to sit and wait, watching, listening, praying the small stuff to God. His presence in my solution is what I need. The fact that the solution has come to me proves He does answer when I call out. I just need to wait and to watch.

Sprouting

While playing cards with friends, I was reminded of the term 'sprouting' in euchre. I learned to play at an early age but wasn't introduced to this concept until college. Sprouting is when some of the points of the scoring cards are partially exposed, thus encouraging them to sprout and grow.

This causes me to pause and think about the game, my life, that I'm involved in. How have I set my scoring cards? Am I playing it safe, or have I exposed some options in my life, encouraging, hoping, waiting for them to grow?

If I make the choice to sprout my points, I encourage my partner to risk more, to gain the upper hand, to call trump, to win the game. When I trust Jesus as my partner, we work as a team.

In the game, I sometimes misjudge, get over-confident, depend on my own abilities to win a round. What happens? EUCHRE! Instead of listening to what my partner does and doesn't say, I bid based on my works, my achievements, my goals. The costs are sometimes painful, sobering.

Still, I play on. This time around, I trust my partner, my Jesus. I allow Him to make the call, the decision. Next thing

I know, He's going alone, wins all five tricks, and we're in the barn! Woohoo!!!

All this odd terminology can confuse one in this game of life. But when I'm partnered with Jesus, sittin' parallel to the bathtub, I'm sure to come out a winner, no matter what hand I've been dealt.

Reunion

I've been surprised by the past. A friend from high school, whom I haven't seen or spoken to for 24 years, contacted me. We had dinner and spent several hours catching up on each other's lives.

Why has this person returned to my life? At first I thought it was to offer him help, but now, I do believe it's the other way around.

Talking with my friend about my faith has made me look it in the eye. I see what I've taken for granted and what I've settled for. I don't want to settle for anything less than what God wants for me. I don't want to do anything less than what He wants me to do.

It's time for me to move on and listen to how God wants me to live for Him. I thought that's what I was doing. I was wrong. I need to let go and allow Him to carry me away.

Want vs. Desire

Want: to be needy or destitute. Desire: to deeply hope or long for. Both speak of intense emotion, a total all-in, I've-got-everything-to-lose gambit. I struggle daily to make a distinction between these overpowering feelings.

For me, there is a difference between want and desire. Want is a temporal thing I can do without. If I don't get a particular thing, if I give it time, something else will pique my interest in its place.

Desire, on the other hand, goes deeper. It strikes at the heart, imbedding into the soul. It has hooks that latch in and hold on. If desire is torn away, it leaves wounds, sometimes little, most often big. The bigger the desire, the bigger the wound.

For a long time, I wanted what is spoken of in fairy tales, a man who would rescue me, causing me to fall in love with him. A typical little girl dream. As my life progressed, that want sat in my life, waiting. Due to lack of fulfillment, other things have replaced it over the years.

Recently, that one-time want returned, transformed into a desire. A desire with more form, more purpose, and more foundation. A desire to share my life with someone who cares for what I care about, to create new hopes and dreams with. A partner who is as passionate about his love of God as I am.

I used to think this would never happen. But God placed in me the wanting for this dream. Now, I see time was needed for me to develop, to grow, to change that particular want into a desire.

God Himself desired me to desire more in a relationship than just to be rescued. He needed me to mature in my relationship with Him, choose to love Him more, so as to prepare me to share my life with another.

I know I'm nowhere close to being ready, but I'm prepared to walk with God through what He gives me. With Him as my desire hooked firmly into me, He will allow other desires to take root, grow, mature and bear fruit. I trust in that.

Longing

What about desire? My heart longs, but is it desire? Would my life be better with the object of my longing? I think it would, as I ponder the feeling in question. But then my mind begins to race down rabbit trails. What if a particular situation happened, then how would I feel? Am I crazy? Do I really think this could happen to me?

Oh how my mind plays tricks with my heart! I see others around me with what I long for and I question if I really am better off without it. I don't know. All I can do is place it at Papa's feet and ask. The worst thing He can tell me is no. If so, I'm not out anything. But if He says yes, my heart leaps in anticipation, in the hope I have been given!

I trust Him to give me what I need in my life, in order to do what He wants me to do. I have to be patient for the answer and know He will let me know in His timing. Yes, I long for my heart's desire to be granted. I also wait to see if it is a true desire and not just a want, a passing fad, a pseudo-feeling that coasts into my mind now and again.

I place my hope in my Papa to give me what I need. I find it interesting when what I want doesn't match up with what He gives me. I also find it is God when they do.

Why?

> *Then God said, "Let us make man in*
> *our image, in our likeness, and let them rule*
> *over the fish of the sea and the birds of the*
> *air, over the livestock, over all the earth, and*
> *over all the creatures that move along the*
> *ground. So God created man in his own*
> *image, in the image of God he created him;*
> *male and female he created them.*
>
> *Genesis 1:26-27*

Why do I long for something I cannot see? Why do I think of things that "might be"? Why do I hope for situations that seem impossible? My only answer is it's in my DNA.

Made in the image of God, could it be that I, too, contain the feelings, the longings, the expectations of my Creator? By experiencing these cravings, these dreams, I get a glimpse of my Father. I realize His desires, His hopes, His "will be." I get to feel His heart beat in anticipation or break in rejection.

He doesn't want me to hurt, but to know Him more sometimes means I have to experience what He goes through. And to think I experience only a grain of sand of His divinity! If I think of my trials magnified a millionfold, I realize the incredible anguish He must endure. But when the joys in my life overflow, oh to imagine the intensity of His joy!

What a burden and a blessing when divinity resides inside my DNA. It's good to know I'm not alone.

Tsunami

Tsunamis devastate lives. They hit when least expected. They don't pick and choose who will be affected. They strike all and take from all. They wash away the stuff of the world and level the playing field. This causes people to rely on others instead of things. They ask for help when they don't know what to do, where to go, how to survive.

My thoughts run wild when I think of everything that has happened lately. A tsunami hit my life last week. The emotional waves raged at me and threatened to drag me under. I cried out for help, physically, spiritually, emotionally. God, my Papa, came and held me, helping me be brave.

I had been praying for rain in my life for several months. I needed to get rid of some things I was hanging onto. I didn't realize they were so deeply entrenched that nothing short of a natural disaster would cause me to let go of them. I never dreamed I would be swept away in a deluge.

But God as my anchor kept me from being washed out to sea. If not for Him, all that makes me who I am would be gone with very slim chance of rescue.

Now the waters have receded and I can see the damage, what is missing, what was destroyed. Picking through the debris is painful, but I'm not left alone to clean up or rebuild. Papa is there to help me, to lift me over the larger pieces, set me down in safer places, protect me from harmful secondary waves.

Talk about the ultimate rescue worker! There could be no better help. Even when things are put to rights to His satisfaction, He stays and oversees the maintenance of this new foundation.

The Wall

Then I said to them, "You see the trouble we are in: Jerusalem lies in ruins, and its gates have been burned with fire. Come, let us rebuild the wall of Jerusalem and we will no longer be in disgrace."

Nehemiah 2:17

I am broken. I look to either side and see shattered remains. Bits here, chunks there. Crumbled evidence of the conquerors who tore me down, breaching me, to take hold of what I protected, what I held sacred, what my existence was for.

I'm no longer a refuge to hide behind. Will I remain in this state, good only for vultures to sit upon to wait for their next meal? Oh, how I long to be rebuilt!

The potential is in my foundation. The laid cornerstone remains true. Be gone, you scavengers of bare bones! The fulfillment of my purpose and the time of my triumph approaches.

I will rise up straight and true to the builder's hand. I will be an imposing presence, a place of solace in an inhospitable land. Those whose hands work at my restoration will be blessed.

As they work to bring back what once was, I will protect them, be their safe haven. I will hold fast to the stone and mortar, the blood and sweat that is shed in my rebuilding. It binds me, heals my wounds, and lifts me up for the glory of my Lord.

Pitfall

How slippery are these walls that surround me! Wet with muck, coated in sludge, there is no purchase for me to grab hold. The more I struggle to rise above the edge of the pit, the dirtier I become. Ankle-deep becomes shin-deep, then knee-deep. Despair descends upon me and I sink down to wallow in the filth at my feet.

Woe is me, how did I get here?! How did I fall into this cesspool? Oh...yeah, I remember now. I stopped looking at my Love, my first love, my true love. I glanced to the side and saw an idol, an ideal, and was mesmerized by its glimmery glitz. I stepped toward it, slipped, and ended up in this place.

Oh, I can get out on my own, I don't need any assistance. If I can just reach out and grab the glamour that dangles above me, I'll be able to escape and everything will be fine. But my efforts don't get me closer to my desire, just deeper into the morass I've allowed to accumulate around me.

So as I slide deeper into the hole, the glimmer fading away, I'm left in the dark, alone, crushed, abandoned. Wallow, wallow, wallow. There is no way out.

Wait! A voice calls out above me! It belongs to my Love, calling to me. He throws down a rope for me. Do I reach out and grab it, knowing He's aware of my tossed-aside affection? I don't deserve His love, but I don't like where I am. I try to climb up the rope, but it's too slippery. Only by tying it around me and allowing Him to lift me out can I be rescued.

As I emerge, coated in grime, He throws His cloak of love over me, in spite of my filthy state. No matter what condition I'm in, He still loves me!

Why did I ever take my eyes, my heart, off Him? Who could ever have compared? Why did I think my plans were better than His? It just goes to show miracles are still performed today. Just look at me.

Touch

Daily I run to Your open arms, knowing You are there, no matter how often I flee from You. You reach toward me, beckoning, encouraging me to come. You offer everything to me, even Your life itself. You weep for me, You fight for me, You comfort me. In essence, You love me!

What do You ask in return? For me to walk with You. You provide my every need. What will I bring? All my worries and cares. They become Yours as long as I keep hold of You. Hold me close so I can hear Your heartbeat, so mine can match it and become steady in its rhythm. Never let me go. Only You can change my world. Thank you for Your touch.

Bagel with a Schmear

*How great is the love the Father has
lavished on us, that we should be called
children of God!*

I John 3:1

I don't know about you, but I enjoy a great-tasting bagel with a huge schmear of cream cheese. My personal favorite is an everything bagel. Top it off with garlic cream cheese and I'm smiling. (Bring on the breath mints!)

The word 'lavish' speaks of heaping, mounding, overflowing, just like I want my schmeared bagel to be. That's what the Father's love does to me. I'm a plain bagel. But then He comes and heaps His flavor-packed affection on me. I'm piled high with His love, oozing over the sides onto others.

He doesn't skimp on His portions, His generosity! In turn, I'm given the opportunity to be generous to those around me. I'm able to share what He has given and rejoice in the joy that spills from me onto others. I know on days when I feel like my bagel is a little dry and lacks flavor, He'll place me next to someone who is overflowing with His schmear of love.

Snow

I sit here, listening to the snow fall around me. As it delicately coats everything in a snug blanket of white, the fall has a gentle, soothing sound. It's subtle, unassuming, beautiful.

God's presence, His love, is like that for me. I wear it as a second skin, fusing it to me so I never need to take it off. I never knew armor could feel so light, yet give the sense of total protection, a completeness.

Here is the invitation. Listen to the snow fall. Open your ears, your mind, your heart, and allow His love to cover you, form around you, and insulate you in His sanctuary.

Crying for Disappointments

How often do I ask for Your assistance, Papa, instead of asking for You? Do I make You my all? I look at recent events in my life and at first I just want to stamp my feet and cry, "No fair!" But then in a flash, I want to fall on my face and proclaim, "Your will be done." I have to let go of what I want and look at what You want, Papa.

You keep telling me how much You love me. Why do I feel I need more? I question myself based on what I perceive others feel about me.

Instead, I must stop and listen to what You say about me. I need to believe it and live it out. You have so much more in store and I need to allow You to show me, take me, grace me with what You choose.

I ask You to bless the disappointments in my life and give them wings to fly. They need room to grow into what You want them to be. Guide me in these disappointments so I check to see if I'm making You my all instead of my assistant.

Blessings

Why don't I ask God for His blessings? That question stops me dead in my tracks. It is true, I don't ask for them. I guess I feel I've already been blessed and if God wants me to have more, He'll give me more.

But should that stop me from posing the question? No! When I ask, I step out to seek Him, to ask for more of Him in my life. Some would call it nagging. I see it as consciously seeking God's will, to allow Him to show more of Himself to me.

When I ask, I'm also made aware of His movement in my life. Sometimes I miss the small ripple that He causes to cross my pond. I don't want to! I want to be consciously aware of His presence as He flows in my life and in other's lives, too. To do this, I have to be active in my pursuit of Him.

This is not to say I don't wait upon His responses. I do wait. I might not see His answers right away, but by expressing my desires to Him regularly, I tell Him I trust His plans will be revealed in due time. Since I haven't been given a specified allotment of blessings, goodness, favor, and desire, I will ask.

What does it hurt to ask? The answer will either be, "Yes," "Not right now," or, "I have better things for you than what you've asked for." I must take the time and ask. I may be surprised by His response.

So here goes. Papa, I ask you to bless me so I may be a blessing to those around me. May I be a sponge that is soaked in Your will and wrung out over others, thus preparing me for a new filling.

Splinters

I've noticed when I get a splinter, it's usually in my hand, a part of the body with a lot of nerve endings, especially in the fingers. When I have a splinter, I become focused on it. I work to get it out, digging, pulling, squeezing.

More often than not, it breaks off and a portion remains under the skin. Now I have to wait. Wait for it to fester enough to be purged. It develops proud flesh, red, hot, and painful.

At times, things in my life are like splinters. Suddenly, something pokes me, impales me as I walk along. So the process of removal begins. I dig at it, only to make it worse. It breaks off and begins to fester, to bother me.

After a while the proud flesh appears. I puff up in defense of this foreign object, even though it hurts. I protect it, cover it. But after a time, my heart tells me it's time to let go of it, to allow it to be cleaned out. Once I permit that to happen, a release comes, and relief covers me in place of the pain, the sensitivity.

When Jesus carried the cross, He was impaled by the splinters of the world. That cross wasn't smooth or clean.

It was covered with our splinters, our sins. He took those into His hands, His shoulders, His heart. The difference with Him is no proud flesh developed. He absorbed the splinters of our lives.

As I reach out to grab the cross, splinters pierce me, only to quickly dissolve in front of my eyes. How amazing! With Jesus in me, He absorbs the splinters of this world that end up in my hands, my heart, and my mind.

What Books
Are in My Library?

> *The thief comes only to steal and kill*
> *and destroy; I have come that they may have*
> *life, and have it to the full.*
>
> *-Jesus*
>
> *John 10:10*

I've come across several entries in my journal regarding fear and its presence in my life, only to stumble across this nugget God empowered me with. *In the face of fear, I close the book. Fear is not a volume I want to read anymore. It holds no truth, no definites, only what-ifs.*

Wow. I didn't realize I had so many books of this genre in my mind's collection. It makes for dreary reading and drearier living. If the only books I have to guide me are about fear, about speculations, how can I base my life, build my life? Talk about putting up hollow walls! When did I give the lies that authored those fears power over me?

Is there a section in my library about travel, about walking through life? Am I allowing God to show me what road to go down, even if it's not one I would choose? I have to stop dwelling on the what-ifs that pop up and trust in His guidance. I need to constantly look to Papa to see where He leads me.

When I look up and follow, the fear is removed and replaced with anticipation. In the anticipation, in the waiting, He reminds me that He has blessed me because He chose me!

This, I know deep in my soul, is truth. Truth is a book I choose to keep in my library, to pick up and peruse daily. Truth is a gift from God, given freely and often. I don't have to wait to re-stock my shelves because new titles on this theme arrive daily. It is a guarantee from Papa, a definite promise lovingly given to me that my life will be full.

Expansion

In Matthew 25, the man buried his talents, what he was given, to preserve or protect them. How often do I do the same with what I've been given? How can God expand my talents, my gifts? Will they grow, enlarge, multiply, if I keep burying them?

The sad thing is that I continuously put new gifts in the same hole with previous ones. Do I hope they will expound to each other their significance? Why is it hard for me to take those gifts, those talents, and make use of them? I'm reminded of a saying about wild animals. "Let it go. If it returns to you, it belongs with you. If it doesn't, it never was yours in the first place."

I need to let my talents go and see where God takes them. I need to change my perspective of acquisition. Instead of holding onto for ownership's sake, I must relinquish for expansion's sake.

Without growth there is stagnation, a sick stillness with a strong possibility of dying and probable death. Take a plant, for instance. It continues to grow constantly. Deprive it of nutrients, water, sunlight, and it will suffer.

How much more will I suffer if I deprive myself of chances to expand? Why do I deny myself the blessing God has for me, my water and sunlight, by not passing on a kind word, a hug, a smile? Are these not basic talents we are all equipped with? When I use my talent to water someone with an uplifting comment, do I not open the door for a reciprocal watering? Yes, and yes again!

Papa, help me dig up the talents I've buried. Help me live in, inhabit, and not possess where you place me every day. It does me no good to protect and preserve something that is dying or dead. As the dust and wind erase, erode away the traces of preservation, I now can treasure what is in front of me instead of what I used to have.

Yes, a precious gift can be treated like a museum piece, kept under glass, cold, sterile, protected. The opportunity to engage it is limited, finite. But when I use my gifts, I allow them to grow into something beneficial. Lord, come expand the talents You've placed in me, in my heart, in my mind.

Pruning

While I visited with a friend who was in the hospital, he reflected on his hospital stays over the years. These periods had given him time to think about God in his life. After he told me an amazing childhood miracle, I shared my own recent reflection on God in my past.

As I think of the trials and struggles I went through in my own childhood, I clearly see His hand on my life. For me to become what God wanted, I had to change. If a tree is sparse, it needs to be pruned. Trim off the dead and sometimes undesirable live growth. From these well-placed cuttings, new growth should appear, expanding the living tree to hopeful, proportional fullness.

I, too, have experienced pruning, and still do. Though at times it is uncomfortable and painful, I wouldn't change things. Even before I asked Jesus into my life, the evidence of His presence was there. That really rocks me, it just blows me away!

I now see where God has pruned me, cut off areas of my life that would have proven detrimental if not downright disastrous. I don't know where I would be if I had chosen to continue on some of the roads that were in front of me.

I think of how God chooses to prune us and what avenues He uses. In spite of his hospitalization, I reminded my friend that God still had a job for him to do, He wasn't done with him yet. He was just going through another pruning. I can't wait to see how he looks come spring, full of new growth as he reaches out into the world around him. Way to grow, Duane!

Campfire Promises from God

The answer I gave you at the campfire is still the same. Look at the log. Does it blaze up right away? No, it must slowly start to catch fire. Soon, the flame moves along the length and begins to consume. Flames don't always appear, but that doesn't mean that heat isn't being given off. Hot coals feed other flames and sustain the fire.

A fire is made up of more than flames. The logs are sustainers of the heat, holding and supporting. They are consumed, but at a slower rate than the twigs or sticks. It doesn't mean they aren't less important because they aren't flashy. They fulfill a different purpose.

Flames will lick about a log to keep going on. Once the flame dies, the coal still is there, smoldering, waiting for the next twig or stick to be placed on it to be consumed and join in the bed of coals. Once flames go out, and they can get smothered easily, coals have to be coaxed to relight them. They have to be blown on, stirred up, fanned to bring forth a flame.

If too much is placed on them, they won't flame. But just the right amount of sticks does the job. The coals glow with new oxygen to bring forth the flame to begin the process anew.

Just remember, when a fire is put out, it requires a lot of water and a lot of stirring to make the coal bed cold. Don't despair when water is thrown on you. It WILL make you sizzle and hiss out. But I will make sure the coal bed is always glowing.

These are My children I watch over and you are among them. Why would I put out such a sparkle of hope, of joy? I won't take away that pleasure of starting new flames in the pit. Have I not shown you this already?

Be at ease knowing the ways will be open and you will know where to walk. This is My choice for you at this time. Abide in it and face forward. Do not look back on what you had. New things are being added to your fire.

Is it more comforting to sit around an unlit fire or around a fire that has been lit for hours? Burn, burn, burn on and worry not about the twigs. Other logs will join you soon and there will be a great rejoicing in My fire.

Broken

I am broken. How much so? It depends on the day. Some days, the cracks are hardly, barely, not at all that visible. On other days, there are gaping holes. It just shows how imperfect a vessel I am.

Jesus shows me my brokenness on a daily basis. Without this revelation, I can't move on and further develop my relationship with Him. It is in this place where He reminds me I can be whole again, fixed, healed of my self-inflicted wounds. I'm restored, eternally glued back together daily with His lifeblood through His sacrifice, His death, and His resurrection.

Only love would, and could, do that.

Recollection

I chose you before I formed you in the womb; I set you apart before you were born. I appointed you a prophet to the nations.

Jeremiah 1:5

How often I forget things. It drives me nuts when I talk to someone and WHOOSH! — what I was saying is gone. I can't seem to retain the thoughts that seem so important.

I try to recall my earliest childhood memories and can't remember much. My baptism is one of them. I know my grandfather performed the ceremony, but I recall nothing. Shouldn't I have some inkling of such a life-changing, momentous time? Then there are some active memories that slowly, gradually swim into focus, to solidify into stories I can retell.

The lack of recall causes me to think about before I was born. Did I know God? Was I with Him, carrying on conversations before I was birthed? What knowledge did my mind contain in that timeframe? When we are born, does God remove our memories of Him, leaving only a tiny seed of recollection that waits to be watered? Will the watering come or will that seed lay dormant?

Since the time my earthly father left this world to join my eternal Father, I've slowly forgotten the sound of his voice. I have a difficult time some days even visualizing his face in my mind.

In contrast, each day brings my eternal Father clearer into focus. New thoughts of Him just seem true. Could it be that I'm beginning to remember the conversations we had before I was born?

Presence

As I sit here in Your sunshine, I'm warmed with Your Presence. You make all the difference in the world. Even though I'm by myself, I'm not alone. You sit beside me and keep me company. Just having the time and opportunity to come outside today is a joy.

Papa, as I sit in Your warmth, open me up to new prospects in my life. Keep me aware of the invitations around me, that I may not pass up these opportunities to impact others.

What is Your plan for me? With the macro zoom of Your camera, bring into focus the possibilities so I may change. I am made more aware of Your presence in many areas of my life.

Lately You've impressed me to be mission-minded in my area of influence. To love and bless, no matter the consequences; to be honest and true to the love You've placed in me, shown me, loved me with.

Garden of the Beloved

Why do I limit my time with You, Papa? I always ask for more of You, but I don't give You my time in return. Walking in a beautiful garden today, You gave me the gift of time to spend in Your presence.

There was so much to see! Your creation of flora on display in complimentary contrasts was breathtaking. As I sat in the shade garden, You enveloped me with the stillness of rejoicing in You.

Is this the serenity that was present with Adam and Eve in the garden? As I imagined You walking down one of the paths to join me on the bench, I was filled with a calm, a hope, an anticipation.

It's good to be in a garden, but it's even more enjoyable to have someone to share it with, to walk with, sit beside, comment on the life that grows around us. Thank you for holding my hand, guiding me as a husband would lead his beloved in a leisurely stroll.

You delight in what causes delight for me. I love You because You know my heart, which in turn, causes me to want to know more of Yours.

Your blessings generate an ache that yearns for only what You can give. That is, You. I humbly submit to Your leadership and ask You to take me on new paths, new adventures in the garden You've grown in me. May my heartfelt desire to give You my everything be a gift You can use for Your purpose!

Invitation

I don't want the stuff of the world to fill me up. If I empty the shelves within me of these things, do I allow God to restock the emptiness inside with what He wants? How often do I allow Him to replenish the shelves in my life? I know I don't do it enough.

In our fast, rush-here, do-this-there society, do I pause, stop, suspend my activity and ask for His quiet presence to come and fill me? I wish I could say I did it more regularly, but that would be a lie. I believe in order for this to happen, I have to be still. Yes, I mean still. I have to be still in my humanness to let God with His divineness in.

His quiet presence, His silence weighs heavy in my mind, heart, soul, pressing me to listen, to pay attention. For what? His voice, love, movement, smell. In these moments of rest, the humanness in me cries out for movement. My leg jiggles back and forth but stops as I pause, showing me how His silence is even more thought-pervasive, more attention-getting than my urge for movement.

The stillness becomes an invitation, a door opened to an empty warehouse, waiting to be filled with Him. I need to ask Him and wait for Him to show up, to bring me new thoughts, feelings, responses. Father, come fill me with Your Spirit, Your Presence, Your Love. Like a store that waits for inventory, I desire You to put new and improved items on my shelves. Restock me with what You have to give so I may open the doors for others to come in and receive.

I tilt my head and listen, still, waiting, hoping. God loves an invitation. Someday, I hope He has a hard time restocking items on my shelves 'cause they're going like hotcakes.

A picture of Him comes to mind. He stands in front of empty shelves, rolls up His sleeves, and looks over to Jesus with an impish grin. Chuckling, He exclaims, "Is this fun or what?!"

My pastor once asked how do you spell love? <u>T-I-M-E</u>. Take time to offer the invitation. Get restocked with His love. The more often, the better. Bust out the walls and expand the store. Wait for new products to hit the shelves! What a sight that will be!

Holy, Holey, Wholly?

As a follower of Jesus, I struggle with my spiritual mentality daily. I don't know if I'm in a minority with this, but it's a truth I can't deny. Each morning, as I brush my teeth to get ready for the day, I ask God for guidance, to show me my place in His story.

But as I get dressed, I sometimes put the world's "spiritual" clothing on instead of His. I exchange the sacred, consecrated, blessed garment of "holy" for the religious, self-righteous, sanctimonious facsimile.

I have a good friend who is a believer of a different spiritual bent. Unbeknownst to him, God has used him to help define, shape, enhance my own personal relationship with God. He's been a great stone to file down my "holy" attitude.

It has made me ponder how we, as believers, easily take the truth of holy and twist it to fit our lives, our world around us.

Personally, I know that by doing so, it becomes convenient for me to continue on, superimposing my beliefs, my platitudes, on others without having to change what I'm doing, how I'm living my life. It's as if I believe that if I can still fit into this particular piece of clothing, I don't need to look in the mirror to see what others see.

One evening, I was talking with a friend about relationships. He spoke about being asked what is it he needed in his life to be complete. Underlying the answer he gave, I could hear him describing the hole in his heart and his attempts to fill it.

Just like my friend, I too, have been trying to fill my heart. As a child, I dreamt of being shot five times in the back with a shotgun. I remember how each impact felt, causing my body to convulse. I now see it's not just one large hole, but multiple punctures.

How many holes are present in my heart? It's like a shotgun has riddled it, perforating it with its destructive force. Just when I think I've allowed God to perform all the needed repairs, a bleeder appears, exposed from its hiding place.

I would think God would get tired of going back in to repair the damage. Fortunately, this is where my relationship with Jesus comes in. His forgiveness, His lovingness, His sacrifice continually beckons me.

When I chose to invite Him to live in me, to love me as holey as I am, He plugged my holey heart from the inside, minimizing the exposure to infection. He asked me to become wholly His.

I know I'm not perfect, nor ever will be until I leave this world. But as long as I have Jesus in my heart, I'm as perfect as I'll ever be until that time. If I have to decide whether to be holy, holey, or wholly, I choose the last. In that choice, I know I'm complete only because of Jesus. As He holds my heart together, I become wholly His, trusting His will, living out what He intended for me.

Purpose

Live your life with purpose.

Dedicate your life to a purpose.

Invite God to re-define your purpose.

Expect Him to train you for your purpose.

Ask others to pray for and over your purpose.

Request His purpose-filled blessing and insights.

Delight in your purpose.

Love with purpose.

Aren't delighted about your purpose yet?

Petition God for a heart transplant in your attitude about your purpose.

Dedicate your children with purpose.

Demonstrate that you trust God will reveal His purpose for their lives to them.

Prayer

Wow, Papa! What conversations I've had lately! Bind my convictions in my spirit, in my soul, in my mind and heart. Hold me up so I may stand in the truth that You've placed in me. I know Your purpose is grand, and I just want to be able to play my role in Your dream, Your ultimate vision.

You have stirred many things in me. Continue to hold me close so I may hear Your heartbeat and risk the glory that is You! You are my goal, my desire, my first and true love.

No worldly love can compare to the love You rain down on me. May I be humble enough to open the floodgates and allow the deluge to flow through to others. May it continue to immerse those around me, spilling over as it spreads. More is what I ask for.

www.ingramcontent.com/pod-product-compliance
Lightning Source LLC
Chambersburg PA
CBHW032018090426
42741CB00006B/642